"Even better than that book I just finished reading about anti-gravity - and just as hard to put down!" - Michael Dadson.

"I read this book not long after I finished that novel about Mount Everest. Talk about a cliffhanger!" - David Fatherington.

"A top, top book. Originally I had plans to read a different book about sinkholes, but they fell through." - Pete Papasley.

The Little Book of

Dad Jokes

A Collection of Dadworthy Funnies

So Bad They're Good

Published by Beartown Press

ISBN 9798649884877

Today, my son asked me, "Can I have a book mark?" and I burst into tears. 11 years old and he still doesn't know my name is Brian.

*

My nickname in my twenties was "The Love Machine". I was really, really bad at tennis.

*

My wife was constantly furious at the fact that I have no sense of direction. In the end I packed up my stuff and right.

*

DAD: "Would you like anything to eat for dinner?" ANYONE: "What are my choices?" DAD: "Yes" or "no".

*

When I was young I was always told to make the little things count. So these days I teach maths to dwarves.

*

My nickname at work is "The Human Compromise". It wouldn't have been my first choice but I'm OK with it.

*

The truth is that 98% of the world is stupid.
Luckily for me, I'm in the other 5%.

*

Have you heard that Post Malone cancelled his tour? They call him Postponed Malone now.

*

I only saw my first porn film last week. I couldn't believe how young I looked.

*

Did I ever tell you about the time I made holy water? I just boiled the hell out of it.

*

Did I ever tell you about when I was in a band called Duvet? We were a cover band.

*

I once bought a pair of shoes from a local drug dealer. I don't know what he laced them with, but I was tripping for the best part of a week.

*

I've started reading a book about anti-gravity. It's simply impossible to put down!

*

I ordered a chicken and an egg on Amazon earlier. I'll let you know.

*

It turns out a slice of apple pie is about $2 in Jamaica and nearly $3 in Trinidad & Tobago. I guess those are just the pie-rates of the Caribbean.

*

Don't you hate when you're waiting at the baggage carousel at the airport, and everyone's luggage is better than yours? Worse case scenario.

*

My wife keeps telling me, "Chin up, it could be worse - you could be stuck in a man-made hole full of water." I know she means well.

*

Even though my friend lost his hair five years ago, he still carries a comb with him to this day. He just can't part with it.

*

It's my wife's birthday this weekend. I've bought her a brand new fridge. I can't wait for her face to light up when she opens it.

*

What do you call a belt made entirely from fifty-pound notes? A waist of money.

*

What do you call a belt made entirely from clock parts? A waist of time.

*

Why is it that you can never tell if there's a psychiatrist in your bathroom? Because their pee is silent.

*

My wife is such a negative Nelly. I remembered the car seat, the pushchair AND the nappy bag. But all she can talk about is how I forgot the baby.

*

I saw a robbery at the Apple store the other day. Apparently they might call on me in court as an iWitness.

*

Did you hear about the invisible man who turned down a job? He couldn't really see himself doing it.

*

What does a pirate say on his 80th birthday?

"AYE MATEY".

*

Oh, guess who I bumped into when I was on my way to get my spectacles repaired? Pretty much everyone.

*

What's the difference between pickled onions and pea soup? Anyone can pickle onions...

*

My wife just tripped and fell while carrying a bunch of clothes she just ironed. All I could do was watch it all unfold.

*

What do storms wear under their trousers?

Thunderpants.

*

A burglar broke in here last night. He said he was looking for money. I got out of bed to look with him.

*

I gave our postman a fright earlier by coming to the door fully nude. I don't know what scared him most, the fact that I was naked or the fact I knew where he lived.

*

What's the best thing about living in Switzerland? I don't know, but I always think the flag is a big plus.

*

My wife told me that she'd leave me if I didn't stop eating so much pasta. Now I'm feeling cannelloni.

*

Did you hear about the cross-eyed teacher? He just couldn't keep his pupils under control.

*

On most weekdays, I wake up grumpy. But at weekends I let her sleep in.

*

What do you call a dog that performs illusions? A Labracadabrador.

*

Five out of four people admit they're bad with fractions.

*

What's Tom Hank's computer password?

"1forrest1".

*

My wife didn't take my name when we got
married. We thought it could get confusing if we
were both called Brian.

*

Every morning when I leave the house, a bike comes out of nowhere and tries to slap me with its handlebars. It's a very vicious cycle.

*

I had to quit my job at the helium plant. I refuse to be spoken to in that tone.

*

ANYONE: "Hey, I was thinking..." DAD: "I thought I smelled something burning."

*

How do you make an octopus laugh? Ten tickles.

*

I'm making a documentary on how planes fly.

We're currently filming the pilot.

*

What did the buffalo say to his son when he

dropped him off at school? Bison.

*

Why do crabs never share? Because they're really

shellfish.

*

To refer to the Elon Musk controversy as "Elon-Gate" seems a bit of a stretch to me.

*

Did you hear about the two peanuts that were walking down the street, minding their own business? One was a salted.

---

*

What's the best way to win a country girl's heart?

A tractor.

*

Albert Einstein may have been a genius, but for me his brother Frank was an absolute monster.

*

What do you call a cow with two legs? Lean beef.

*

What do you call a cow with no legs? Ground

beef.

*

What do you call a cow with a twitch? Beef jerky.

*

My wife finds a man in camouflage a huge turn-on. I just don't see it.

*

I said to the waitress, "Can I ask you something about the menu please?" She slapped me across the face. To be fair, the men she pleases are none of my business.

*

Did you hear about the guilty dolphin who kept getting off in court? They finally put him away for crimes against a manatee.

*

I think I really connected with my inner self today. That's the last time I use cheap toilet paper.

*

I just watched a documentary about beavers. It was the best dam show I ever did see.

*

ANYONE: "Did you get a haircut?" DAD: "No, I got them all cut!"

*

What's the loudest pet? A trumpet.

*

Did I tell you about the velcro I bought last

week? It was a total ripoff.

*

I'm putting on a fundraising event next week for people who struggle to climax. Let me know if you can't come.

*

I can only ever recall 25 letters of the alphabet. I don't know why.

*

When I was a lumberjack, I felled exactly 6,418 trees. I know that because I kept a log.

*

I've got a joke about a thin piece of paper, but it's pretty tearable.

*

My teenage daughter treats me like a god. She acts like I don't exist until she wants something.

*

Does Sean Connery like herbs? He does, but only partially.

*

What's big, grey and just doesn't matter? Irrelephant.

*

My neighbour was in his garden the other day.

He shouted over to ask what I knew about bonsai

trees. I shouted back, "Very little".

*

Did you know that if you rearrange the letters of

"postmen", they get really annoyed?

*

Did you hear about the man who invented Polos?

They say he made a mint.

*

What do prisoners use to stay in touch? Cell

phones.

*

You know what makes me throw up? A

dartboard on a ceiling.

*

What do sprinters eat before a race? Nothing,

they fast.

*

Why did the cow win a trophy? Because he was

simply outstanding in his field.

*

Why couldn't the bicycle stand up by itself? It was two-tired.

*

I once went to a job interview where they asked me if I could perform under pressure. I said no, but I'd have a decent crack at I Want to Break Free.

*

Do you know what I think is the most groundbreaking invention of all time? The shovel.

*

Why can't a hand be 12 inches? Because it'd be a foot.

*

People say I'm a bad winner, but fortunately I've now been prescribed anti-gloating cream. I just can't wait to rub it in.

*

I grew up in a rough neighbourhood. As a child people would cover me in chocolate, cream and put a cherry on my head. It was tough in the gateau.

*

Where's the best place in America to buy a soccer kit? New Jersey.

*

I went to a restaurant on the moon once. Great food, no atmosphere.

*

I went to a wedding of two satellites. The ceremony wasn't much, but the reception was incredible.

*

Why do melons tend to have grandiose weddings? Because they cantaloupe.

*

How many apples grow on a tree? All of them

grow on a tree.

*

Have you heard that rumour about butter? Well,

I'm not going to be the one to spread it.

*

How do you make a waterbed even bouncier? Fill
it with spring water.

*

Why do you never see hippos hiding in trees?
Because they're so good at it.

*

I was burgled by six dwarves last week. Not
happy.

*

My wife tells me I have two major faults; that I
don't listen, and something else.

*

How does a polar bear construct his house?

Igloos it together.

*

Why did the old man fall in the well? Because he couldn't see that well.

*

To whoever stole my brand new copy of Microsoft Office, I will track you. You have my Word.

*

I once had a summer job in a shoe-recycling

shop. It was sole-destroying.

*

They told me I'd never be good at poetry because

I'm dyslexic. But so far I've made three bowls

and a Toby jug and they're all lovely.

*

My boss told me to have a good day. So I went
home.

*

I once thought about going on an all-almond
diet... But it would just have been nuts.

*

50

My wife was telling me for ages that I had to stop acting like a flamingo. In the end I had to put my foot down.

*

I told my wife she'd drawn her eyebrows far too high up on her forehead. She looked surprised.

*

My uncle named his dog Big Rolex. He was a watch dog.

*

Two goldfish are in a tank. One says to the other, "So, do you know how to drive this thing?"

*

What do you call an undercover noodle? An impasta.

*

I've been bored recently so I've decided to take up fencing. The neighbours say they're going to call the authorities unless I put it back.

*

I think my wife keeps dropping glue on my antique firearm collection. She denies it but I'm sticking to my guns.

*

I know a lot of jokes about retired people but none of them work anymore.

*

What's orange and sounds like a parrot? A carrot.

*

What's ET short for? Because he's only got little legs.

*

I recently found a black, circular piece of plastic. It had a little hole in the middle and came in a cardboard sleeve. I picked it up and threw it like a frisbee. It flew for more than 100 yards. I'm sure that must be a record.

*

Why do carp always sing a little bit off-key? You can't tuna fish.

*

I just got hired at a company that makes bicycle wheels. I'm the spokesperson.

*

A storm blew away about a quarter of my roof last night. Oof.

*

I somehow made it through high school while only being able to remember even numbers. What are the odds?

*

I just found out that "Aaaaaarghhh" is not a real word. I can't express how angry I am.

*

Where do bad rainbows get sent to? Prism.

*

What do you call a magician who has lost his magic? Ian.

*

How many bones are in a human palm? Just a
handful.

*

I recently swapped around all of the labels on my
wife's spice rack... She hasn't noticed yet, but I
know the thyme is cumin.

---

*

How do you row a kayak filled with puppies? You bring out the doggy paddle.

*

I worked for a bank but I got fired in my first week. This woman asked me to check her balance, so I pushed her over.

*

Personally, I don't trust staircases one little bit.

They're always up to something.

*

I don't know about you, but I hate jokes about

German sausages. They're just the wurst.

*

What lies at the bottom of the ocean and bites

its fingernails? A nervous wreck.

*

How do you organize an astronomer's party?

You planet.

*

What do you call a fish with no eyes? A fsh.

I used to be really keen to get a job cleaning mirrors. It was the only thing I could really see myself doing.

What's the most common cause of divorce?

Marriage.

*

Why did the cyclops have to close his college?

Because he only had the one pupil.

*

Why did the coffee call the authorities? It got

mugged.

*

How do you think the unthinkable? You uthe an

itheberg.

*

Cosmetic surgery used to be kind of taboo, but talk about Botox now and no one raises an eyebrow.

*

I have the world's most terrible thesaurus. Not only is it terrible, but it's also terrible. And terrible.

*

Why do seagulls usually fly over the sea?
Because if they flew over the bay, they'd be
called bagels.

*

What's brass and sounds like Tom Jones?
Trombones.

*

What's the difference between Prince Charles
and a juggling ball? One's heir to the throne,
the other's thrown in the air.

*

What did the wimpy grape do when someone
trod on it? It let out a little wine.

*

What's the difference between a hippo and a Zippo? One is heavy and one is just a little lighter.

*

To be frank, I'd have to change my name.

*

What's blue and not all that heavy? Light blue.

*

Why can't those selfish hedgehogs just share the hedge?

*

What do you call an introverted alligator in a vest? A private investigator.

*

What do you get when you cross a fish with

two elephants? Swimming trunks.

*

If you want to get a job working in the

moisturiser business, the best advice I can give

is to apply daily.

*

I gave all of my dead batteries away earlier

today... Free of charge.

*

I went to the corner shop earlier... Came home

with four corners.

*

Last Saturday my wife and I watched three films back-to-back. Fortunately, I was the one facing the TV.

*

I've just been diagnosed as colourblind. It completely came out of the green.

*

Sorry, I was just thinking about the reverse gear in my car. It really takes me back.

*

A cat, a dog and a fish walk into a bar. The fish suffocates.

*

I wrote a song about tortillas earlier. Actually, it

was more of a rap.

*

What do you call a bee that's based in

America? A USB.

*

I bought my wife a castle that can do maths.

She doesn't particularly like it, but it's the fort

that counts.

*

What's Whitney Houston's favourite type of

coordination? HAND

EEEEEEEEYYYYEEEEE!

*

I bought a ceiling fan the other day. Total waste of money. He just stands there applauding it and saying, "Ooh, I love how smooth and high it is".

*

A farmer asked me if I could help him round up 28 cows. I said, "Yes, of course - that's 30 cows."

*

I accidentally booked myself on this escapology

workshop. Now I'm really struggling to get out

of it.

*

Every so often, I tuck my knees into my chest,

lean forward and let momentum do the rest.

That's just the way I roll.

*

Why is your door not completely a door?

Because sometimes it's ajar.

*

I used to work at a calendar factory but I got
sacked for taking a few days off.

*

I was once burgled, but all the two thieves took
was a calendar. It was OK in the end. They
each got six months.

*

I've been happily married for three years – out of a total of eight.

*

I'm terrified of lifts... but from now on I'm taking steps to avoid them.

*

I used to hate sideburns… but then they grew
on me.

*

Ever tried to eat a clock? It's very time-
consuming. (And you wouldn't go back for
seconds.)

*

I go down but never up. What am I? A yo.

*

What's the best selection of insects to rent a flat

out to? Ten ants.

*

What do you call a boomerang that doesn't

come back? A stick.

*

What do you call a fly without wings? A walk.

*

I saw an advert in the newsagents: "TV for sale,
£3, volume stuck on full blast". I thought,
"There's no way I'm turning that down".

*

Have you seen that new corduroy pillow they're selling now? It's really making headlines.

*

Just received a birthday card full of rice. It's from Uncle Ben.

*

My old boss died last week. He was hit by a falling piano. They think it'll be a low key funeral.

*

I saw this documentary on how ships are kept together. Riveting.

*

I once had a job where I drilled holes for water

all day long – it was well boring.

*

My grandfather once told me I should invest

my money in bonds. So I bought 50 DVDs of

Casino Royale.

*

I went to the local bookshop and asked the woman behind the desk if I could buy a book about turtles. She said "Hardback?" and I said, "Yeah, and tiny little heads".

*

How do you sell a cow to someone who's hard of hearing? *leans in close and shouts* HEY, YOU WANNA BUY A COW???!

*

Before I met my wife I used to date this girl who had a lazy eye. But it turned out she was seeing somebody else the entire time.

*

What's green and has three foreheads? Grass, I lied about all the foreheads.

*

How heavy was Buddha? Not very. He'd been enlightened.

*

ANYONE: I'm cold. DAD: Go and stand in that corner. It's 90 degrees over there.